*Gifts from Guidance is a present from spirit
delivering love
straight to your heart.*

Gifts *from* Guidance

A Book of Prayers and Affirmations Offering Comfort,
Encouragement, and Possibility as We Create Our Daily Lives

KAY CHRISTY, MA

BALBOA
PRESS

A DIVISION OF HAY HOUSE

Cover Art Mosaic created by Jennifer Kuhns, Mosaic Artist
Architectural and fine art mosaic with a focus on sustainability
www.JKMosaic.com

Balboa Press books may be ordered through booksellers or by contacting:
Balboa Press
A Division of Hay House
1663 Liberty Drive
Bloomington, IN 47403
www.balboapress.com
1 (877) 407-4847

Because of the dynamic nature of the Internet, any web addresses or
links contained in this book may have changed since publication and
may no longer be valid. The views expressed in this work are solely those
of the author and do not necessarily reflect the views of the publisher,
and the publisher hereby disclaims any responsibility for them.

The author of this book does not dispense medical advice or prescribe the use
of any technique as a form of treatment for physical, emotional, or medical
problems without the advice of a physician, either directly or indirectly. The
intent of the author is only to offer information of a general nature to help
you in your quest for emotional and spiritual well-being. In the event you use
any of the information in this book for yourself, which is your constitutional
right, the author and the publisher assume no responsibility for your actions.

Printed in the United States of America.

ISBN: 978-1-4525-8998-5 (sc)
ISBN: 978-1-4525-9000-4 (hc)
ISBN: 978-1-4525-8999-2 (e)

Library of Congress Control Number: 2014900540

Balboa Press rev. date: 3/26/2014

Contents

Dedication

For my precious girl and her precious girl.

May you always find the essence of me in these pages.
I am love,
I am whole,
I am complete

    because of you.

Gifts from Guidance

There is a place in our inner landscape
that knows only of wholeness, and love, and faith.

When we meet in this place
the possibilities of life are endless,
the solutions appear with brilliant light and clarity.

Follow a path or a meandering river to find this land
and stay true to the song of your own heart.

The guides speak only of love
and possibility
and infinite joy.

Holding the highest truth and deepest love
as you journey forward.

Listen to the space between your breaths,
become lovers with quiet and calm,
taste the colors of nature,
then... soar above it all and see perfection.

We meet in this spirit-filled space
and offer gifts of wealth and jewels for love;
staff and crowns and robes for peace.

You are majestic,
royal,
whole,
and unique.

Be guided to your gifts with ease and grace.

Preface

December 12, 2012

Today I am able to see the end, the accomplishment of my goal of writing a book of prayers and affirmations. Therefore, today is a good day to write about the beginning.

I was born in the Iowa summer of 1955, under the Cancer sun and Virgo moon, the fourth and last child of a Midwest family with roots in farming and small business ownership.

There are two things I have always loved about the season and place of my birth. Being born in late June, just after the summer solstice, and true to the traits of an astrological Cancer, I easily recognize and access my emotions and the emotions of others. I have always loved people and people watching. In addition to being attuned to emotion, from a young age I was able to perceive the experiences of others easily. As I grew older, I began to understand this as a gift and something precious and true about me. These attunement skills have been primary to my professional endeavors and educational choices.

Being born in Iowa to a family whose patriarchal heritage was farming, I notice the land, the animals, and the birds. I understand the importance of conservation and feel the changing of the seasons in the colors, sounds and rhythms of nature. I have a keen sense for what the farmers are doing, even though I have never farmed. My cultural roots are Iowan, and in my heart of hearts, I am a farm girl.

As a teenager I discovered my ability to anticipate the needs of others, sometimes at my own expense. In these developmental years I began my lifelong journey to understanding balance and boundaries. Capable of true empathy and compassion, I was the friend to call to discuss emotions and relationships. I am an empath, and coaching others from this place of deep caring is one of my gifts.

I married young, had a daughter at age nineteen, left the heartland, and moved to the Pacific Northwest. It was the '70s! I was young and a seeker, and although I loved being a young wife and mother, I was hungry to learn more about offering useful counsel to others.

When I was in my late twenties, I met a gypsy woman who exposed me to "fortune-telling" using a deck of playing cards. I had never experienced anything like it, and after my first card reading I was hooked. I wanted to learn everything I could, and that hunger for knowledge still guides me today. She taught me to access my intuition and then taught me to perform card readings for other people. This began a new chapter of translating my natural talents into trusting my psychic and intuitive abilities, with the intention of offering guidance and support to others while also discovering my higher self.

I have journeyed through decades of career development, education, parenting, divorce, maturity, and self-discovery. Along the way I have taken classes in metaphysics and worked with astrologers, intuitive readers, spiritual directors, palmists, mediums, and numerologists as a course of study toward personal and spiritual development. I have also used the principles of twelve-step programs and the teachings of religious science to shape my beliefs.

When I was in my early forties, I learned the techniques of automatic writing, and began to practice it daily. The writing became another unique gift I could use privately as a meditative practice and a way to access my highest self. I also began to use automatic writing with clients as a spiritual coaching tool. It was during this period of my life that prayers and affirmations began to come to me in the writing.

The prayers and simple affirmations in this book come from a writing process that is delivered through me but is not from me alone. I hear words, see pictures, and write from a place of connection to my personal guidance system – my unique GPS – which includes guides, angels, and loved ones who have passed from their earth life. This committee of helpers – or, as I sometimes write, my tribe of love – has overseen the creation of this book and the launching of my business, Spirit Led Life Company.

Today, in my sixth decade of life, I continue to build on the simple foundation of my upbringing and my innate gifts. I still occasionally read the playing cards, but automatic writing is my love and my way of speaking directly with my spirit guides.

It has taken years for me to find the words to describe this work and to develop the confidence to bring it forward. As the number of people who request these prayers has grown, it has become clear to me that these prayers are healing and can be life preservers of peace and hope at times of stress, uncertainty, and fear.

They are gifts from my unique guidance system, and I offer them to you. I hope you will use them and make them your own.

The guided writing has changed me.
Softened me.
Brought me to my highest good and kindest self.
It is my hope that these prayers will do the same for you.

Words are inadequate to express the gratitude I feel for this gift
and the love and joy I feel as I offer it to you.

Thank you.

This prayer was given to me verbally by the woman who first taught me intuitive and psychic development in 1979. Her ethnicity was gypsy, and she had been taught this prayer by her grandmother. It did not come with a title or reference to an author. As far as I know, it was passed down verbally woman to woman, generation to generation.

For thirty-five years I have used this prayer to bring my thoughts and emotions in alignment with spirit. Using this prayer is where my belief, curiosity, and commitment to prayer began. I believe using it daily has led me to the life I live today.

I gave it the title "Spiritual Practice Prayer" as I began to use it with clients.

Spiritual Practice Prayer

All persons, places, things, thoughts, and activities
that are <u>not </u>a part of my divine plan,
<u>release me now</u>.

<u>I release from me now</u>
all persons, places, things, thoughts, and activities
that are <u>not</u> a part of
my divine plan.

<u>I call to me now</u>
all persons, places, things, thoughts, and activities
that <u>are</u> a part of
my divine plan.

Introduction

The Gift of Automatic Writing

In the 1990s, I attended a class titled *Working with Your Angels*. It was taught by a woman who described herself as an angel reader. She performed individual readings for clients during which she acted as a vehicle for people to meet and communicate with their spirit guides and angels.

Meeting her marked an exciting phase of my spiritual development. It was time to put into practice the culmination of what I had learned through years of study and from my own intuitive and guided readings.

The class was a study in the universal truths of angels and their wisdom in tandem with daily practice in spiritual growth techniques. In this class I learned to craft my own affirmations. I had read the work of Louise Hay, Marianne Williamson, and Shakti Gawain but had yet to realize these techniques as my own, to use them to craft phrases and affirmations that would enhance my unique life.

I began by writing sentences to invoke the support of my guides and angels and then watched for the subtle signs that higher guidance was operating in my life. I purchased white three-by-five inch index cards and wrote one statement per card as study aids for manifesting and receiving guidance.

As a student with a skeptical nature, I began with simple sayings to see what happened. I carried the cards in my car and daily planner in order to read them over and over again throughout the day. Some examples of the progression of the early phrases follow:

* I ask for your help and guidance to _____ I filled in the blank with anything from "find a parking spot" to "heal an injured back."

* I ask for the ability to love myself as the most important love in my life.

* Then I wrote single statements, always beginning with "I" and written as if the thing I requested had already arrived.
  o I have all the love in the universe!
  o I am at peace.
  o My body is perfection.
  o I am a spiritual being (with a human body).
  o I am loved unconditionally.
  o I am never alone.
  o I accept myself *exactly* as I am.
  o I am enough.
  o I trust myself.
  o All is as it should be.
  o I believe I am a part of GOD.

I began to notice my usual negative or unhappy thought patterns were being interrupted. I also found I could change the experience of my day to a happier, more positive one by asking for assistance and then following the signs and messages I was given.

I grew to call these "sticky-note phrases" because I handwrote them on sticky notes and put them all around the visual walls of my world to assist me in catching and adjusting my own thought patterns. I love the phrases for their simplicity and for the foundational truth they deliver to my day. At times of personal stress, these are still the first tool I use to adjust my thoughts.

The work with my own guides progressed, and I began to use automatic writing to deepen this spiritual communication. When the first glimpses of automatic writing came through me, the process seemed easy and special, a beautiful way to bring forward the deepest truth of me. It was becoming clear to me that the intuitive writing process was invoking messages through my highest self that were brought by my spirit guides and guardian angels. A progression was occurring and I began to receive phrases in the writing process that I knew were not from my own thoughts.

At first I could not hold the connection easily; the phrases would come quickly, and then the spiritual connection would end. I wrote with my nondominant hand and with my eyes closed. When I opened my eyes and saw words on the page (usually going downhill), I was thrilled. Where did these words and messages come from? I was not sure, but loving the process, I kept going.

Over time I could tune to this vibration and use my dominant writing hand. Then, slowly, I could open my eyes and keep writing. My guides and guardian angels began to introduce themselves in the writing, and my fascination and commitment grew quickly.

I often began a writing session by asking for assistance in diminishing anxiety and worry, especially about one of three things: money matters, a love relationship and being a good mother to my adult daughter, my three personal favorite worry routines!

It was a delicate process. I lost the threads of awareness and connection to my higher self easily, partially because I would become so excited by what was happening. The first affirmations and prayers I wrote were for me. Then I began to receive them for my closest friends. They came to me when one of us was suffering, and there was nothing that comforted or relieved the pain of deceit, anxiety, heartache, or fear.

What follows are some of my favorites, the ones I come back to over and over when I find myself in need of spiritual comfort and encouragement. I hope you will use them – or better yet, use them as examples to craft your own that are personal and unique to your life's journey.

Everything
is in divine and perfect order,
right here,
right now.

I am ready
and embrace each new opportunity
delivered to my life
as destiny unfolding.

I accept good graciously into my life.
All of my needs are met abundantly,
now and always.

I am alive.
I am GOD.
I love myself.
Love is not lost.
I attract love, as I am love.
So be it!

———————————

I know who I am.
I know what I want.
My heart's desire lives in me.

———————————

I offer myself to the highest good.
May I be comforted by knowing
my divine plan is unfolding perfectly.
I am safe.
I am calm.
I am free.

———————————

My life is unfolding perfectly.
The pace is correct for all involved
as I learn patience, clarity,
and communication of my true self.
I practice boundaries.
I understand love.
I know what I want.

———————————

I am whole.
I am content.
I have faith in goodness and love.
I am guided and protected in all I do.

—————————————

Today I fully accept who I am and how I feel.
I am love.
I am enough.
My imperfections are a perfect expression of GOD.

—————————————

I release this relationship to GOD and the angels.
May it be transformed to match our highest good.
Please show me the way.

—————————————

Please show me
the right actions to take
to generate financial abundance.

—————————————

Ask. Accept. Receive.
I know who I am.
I have all I need.
I love easily and effortlessly.

—————————————

I am ready to receive.
I relax
and ask for all my bills to be paid
effortlessly and easily.

━━━━━━━━━━━━━━━━━━

The time has come.
The time is now.
Release.
Step back.
Watch abundance unfold.

━━━━━━━━━━━━━━━━━━

The right employment has arrived.
It supports me both financially and at a soul level.

━━━━━━━━━━━━━━━━━━

I know who I am.
I have everything I need
to experience love,
to be love,
to have love.

━━━━━━━━━━━━━━━━━━

My body supports me fully.
I am pain-free and move through life easily.
I am flexible and strong
and filled with joy.

━━━━━━━━━━━━━━━━━━

I manifest love and sexual satisfaction
as I grow in patience, kindness, boundaries, and desire.
I know what I want.
I trust GOD to provide the means for how.
As I know
I shall have.

I am healing.
I am moving forward.
I accept the truth and embrace opportunities to learn and grow.
Universal timing is perfect timing.

I understand this writing to be divinely guided and I also know it is uniquely me. Advancing from the sticky-note phrases to these longer affirmations, I noticed themes and patterns emerging. There was language of universal love and truth that was not how I normally spoke or thought. This language increased my belief that I was connecting to my highest self, the place of spirit consciousness that wants only love, peace, and joy for all. Doing this work began to heal my self-esteem wounds, and as I shared the affirmations with others, they reported experiencing their own healing.

The feedback and encouragement from friends and family kept me motivated, and I started to write more for others, including people I did not know well and those I did not know at all. This was the beginning of the longer prayers emerging through the automatic writing process and the advent of my ability to offer this technique to clients in my professional life-coaching practice.

As the longer prayers began to come through, they had a repeating cadence and symmetry. Images and phrases often came in triple: three words, three phrases, three stanzas.

I found this "tripling" interesting because my first love of poetry was haiku, which my sister taught me when I was junior high school age. Haiku is written in three lines in a syllabic sequence of five, seven, five. I still love the discipline required in meeting the syllable requirements and the seasonal reference that is typical in traditional Japanese haiku.

My sister and I often wrote haiku to each other in greeting cards, e-mail, and personal notes attached to gifts. When our lives were separated by physical distance, and computer-based methods of communication became more readily available, we developed a method of communication via e-mail that I loved. One of us would begin by writing and sending a haiku via e-mail. The other would copy one line or riff off of a line in a similar tone and write a new haiku from it. Back and forth we went until the story of our day or our life was told.

I am sharing this history of story and poetry in my family because I think it helps explain how this all began for me. The cadence of this writing style has been in me always, taught to me by my sister and to her by my poet brother during their college years.

These poems/prayers have been easy to access and accept because I come from a family of writers and poets. I also come from a generation for whom beautiful words were crafted in greeting cards and given to mark the highs and lows of life.

We were a family with six members, who gave poems and short stories as gifts, pieces that captured our sorrows, apologies, and congratulations to each other.

My mother cut poems, prayers and *Peanuts* comic strips out of *Reader's Digest* and other magazines and tucked them everywhere. Prayers and poems were tucked into her journals, her cookbooks, and her little boxes of pens, postage stamps, and paper clips. My maternal grandmother copied prayers into her recipe books.

My father used writing to speak his deepest truth. When he had something important to say, it always came in the form of a heartfelt letter of love, advice, or recommendation. A framed poem hangs in my home that my father wrote as a gift to me during a family vacation in 1974. It is a precious and treasured memory of his love for me even now, forty years later.

Prayer Writing

As I study spiritual development and spiritual thought leaders, I recognize similarities between my words and those of many other practitioners. These similarities have helped me to understand the spiritual and universal nature of these prayers and of the writing gift I have been given.

When I am in the automatic-writing process, I am only partially aware of the words. I hear them and write them as unique sentences or phrases. When the writing is complete and I reread it in its totality, the message of the piece is often new to me.

Today I can easily move in and out of the space that is necessary to hear my guides and highest knowing. There were times when I did not know, and then would forget, to ask my guides to stop talking and found myself over-sensitive to everything around me, especially when I was in public places or large gatherings of people, where there was so much energy I found it hard not to pick up on the thoughts and experiences of strangers.

With practice it became easy to disconnect from the stories of others unless asked, which was a great relief. I had a much harder time disconnecting from the intense emotional experiences of my family and friends, whether they were asking for my interpretations and intuitive input or not.

Writing prayers helps me to separate from the existential suffering of those I love. It is how I offer comfort, encouragement and hope to my loved ones without becoming enmeshed in their experience.

In my life the events that caused this level of suffering came in the form of shocking relationship betrayals, news that a death had occurred, loss of health and mobility, a reality-shattering accident, and knowledge that the clarity and connection to one I loved had been lost to addiction.

In the lives of my friends and clients, they came as the death of a family member, miscarriage, divorce, and business failure. When these types of events occur there is nothing to say to relieve the heartache,

So I wrote prayers...
Because I had to...

and because I was desperate to find my own relief and had been brought to my knees in surrender. In these moments connection to spirit was the only solution for me.

The opening prayer in the Comfort chapter is one of the early prayers that came to me. I used it to interrupt the thought cycles of pain and worry that were running in my head on auto-play. I was suffering over a relationship and was in search of peace and a higher purpose.

Each time I noticed this auto-play running in my thoughts, I inserted the prayer. When I could not remember it, I went back to my early training and wrote it on three-by-five inch index cards. Again, I surrounded myself with the messages: in my wallet, on the dashboard of my car, on my computer, on my bathroom mirror, and above the kitchen sink.

I was both humbled and amazed by the process, first because of how often I caught myself running a fear fantasy through my head. I didn't even hear my own thoughts, let alone understand what I was saying in the recesses of my mind.

Once I began to have the awareness, humility was all I could access because I was stunned by the quantity of time I spent in fear and self-hatred.

It seemed like thousands of times a day I slowed down to interrupt a thought and inserted a prayer, an affirmation or a sticky-note phrase. The prayers pulled me from fear, worry and loathsome thoughts about myself. This process was a spiritual awakening for me because I began to feel personal relief and to believe I could offer the same relief to others with this writing gift.

Many of the prayers in the Comfort chapter are my earliest work. They were written with the intent to offer comfort during times of life challenge, disappointment, and heartache – my own and those of my friends and clients.

Many of them were written to soothe anxiety, worry, and fear. I never questioned that they came to me as a gift from my inner guidance system, and I was able to offer them freely to others as gifts to their souls and psyches.

However, the spiritual development I was nurturing became problematic for me. The collision of active codependence in a love relationship with spiritual laws and practices created tremendous tension and confusion.

As I became proficient at intuitive writing, I asked about the relationship. Because I was tuning to my spirit guides for data, the words I received were loving, beautiful and descriptive of a soul connection across lifetimes, a connection that I felt and knew to be true but was not experiencing in daily life. The affirmations and prayers that came through during the later years of the relationship saved my life.

I was drowning in pain and feeling tremendous pressure from living this double life – remaining connected to and feeling responsible for a man who was held in the grips of an addiction so intense that it seemed to be his only true love. I knew no fix for his addiction, no way to compete with it, and no way to elevate my life to a higher vibration of happiness.

At the same time, I was growing in my abilities to write prayers for myself and others that were beautiful and helpful and that came from a place of true and absolute love. I was living an oxymoronic life, and no amount of denial kept the truth at bay.

My self-esteem crisis was reaching a tipping point and my daughter was pregnant with my first grandchild. It was time for me to walk through the gates of life and embrace elder status, to accept the crone and goddess energy that I could feel and taste in my being. I was born to be an exceptional grandmother, and I was ready. Grandmothering is a perfect place to focus a natural talent for codependence in a healthy way. Hallelujah! I had reached nirvana.

Except for the man who I periodically invited back into my home and my heart. I wanted him to find health and happiness with *me* and allowed this desire to create havoc for us both. The writing gift was how life showed me with brilliant clarity the crossroads I had approached.

To become the woman I was meant to be, I would need to step into a higher order of living. This step would require a complete detachment to achieve the wholeness that I wanted and could begin to see, but I would have to walk toward it without reservation.

In the spring of 2012, I was riddled with fear and anxiety to a degree that I had never before experienced. I was taking anxiety medication shortly after waking each morning. I arose with a feeling of dread and doom that I could not shake; partnered with the sense that panic would arrive at any moment. Mental health therapy, along with chiropractic care, acupuncture, and massage therapy, kept me propped up and functioning… barely.

And then I quietly and methodically took a stand for myself.

* My work in state government had waned, and I was being asked to perform tasks that were not in alignment with my soul's work. I took an opportunity to leave my job and completed a career cycle working as an internal organization development practitioner and executive coach.
* I left the relationship with my beloved "Marlboro man" with a finality that even I knew was real.
* My daughter and my granddaughter, who had been living with me during a transition in my daughter's life, moved to their own home.

In the span of one month, I became the hero of my own life. I changed or allowed to change almost everything about my daily routine – by my own design.

I sat in liminal space for many months. Joan Borysenko defines liminal space as "that time between what is no longer and what is not yet" and that is exactly what I was living. I spent my time cleaning drawers and closets, taking walks, assembling jigsaw puzzles, grandparenting, sleeping, gardening, writing, thinking, resting and reading until the cocoon phase was complete. The transformation had begun, and I was ready to reemerge, refreshed and sparkling again.

I transformed to a different way of life. I used prayer and spiritual practice to illuminate a new path, an easier road, a brilliant life that is custom-made for my true essence.

Today, I am happy and grateful every day, even on the cloudy days. My future unfolds daily in ways that are better than the thoughts and ideas I have, so I often step aside and listen with new ears to the suggestions life offers. I do not know the details of my future, such as where will I live, what my next career will be, from which direction financial stability will arrive, or whether the new love will come in the afternoon or the evening.

Through the writing, the practice of spiritual techniques, and trusting in the power of positive thinking and love, I live primarily in the realm of possibility.

I know my life will ebb and flow through periods of needing comfort and encouragement again, as that is the river in which I swim – downstream now, in the natural flow of the current, floating and laughing and changing direction when the raft gets hung up on low branches and rocks.

I end this section with a haiku.

I am free and blessed.
Love is my compass today.
Water over rock.

My Intent in Sharing the Prayers

Many authors have written about positive thinking. My first exposure to these concepts occurred when I was a teenager. My father, an insurance sales manager, had been sent to a seminar given by Norman Vincent Peale and he came home with a copy of Peale's book, *The Power of Positive Thinking*.

I know my dad studied this work and the work of Dale Carnegie as he polished his talent for sales. He was a master at combining the core concepts of selling with positive thinking as his signature style. He raised me to believe that positive thinking was necessary to create a successful sales career, but I did not make the leap to positive thinking being necessary for a happy life until much later.

My mother was a Presbyterian who used prayer and religious study to calm her nerves and explain the unexplainable, particularly the unexplainable bad stuff like alcoholism, hysteria, fear, mental illness, and rage. She was private about her true beliefs, but I always knew that saying a prayer and asking God for help was a balm to her soul. She quietly and methodically created a community of church women as her friends, confidantes, and bridge partners.

I believe that on some level, this book began as an acknowledgement to my mother and the women she loved and cared for through prayer. Her requests of God were not overt, but they were never far from our dining room table or her private sanctuary.

The prayers offered in this book are divided into three chapters: Comfort, Encouragement and Possibility. As I began to organize them for publication, these three words – comfort, encouragement, and possibility – emerged as repeating themes.

The prayers of the Comfort section were born from human suffering. They were written from my soul's desire to ease my own suffering and then the suffering of those I love. Others have always sought me out for comfort, for a compassionate ear, and for advice, yet in the darkest shadows, it is only spirit that can lift a mood and offer an alternative to pain.

The prayers of the Encouragement section come as the first glimmer of hope, a bit of light shining through to say the suffering may have an ending point. We notice our bodies taking a breath. Standing in this hope also creates a connection to that power in the universe that is greater than one human being. This power can heal us, transform our heartaches, and lead us to creativity and lightness.

When the suffering that only comfort can ease has begun to diminish, the prayers of encouragement emerge. Get up from the recliner and take a walk. Leave the house to take a swim. Go to the grocery store and notice the people and the colors of the sky. It is time for encouragement.

There are many prayers in the Encouragement section that honor and invoke the seasons. As I stated in the Preface, I am connected to the land and the seasons. The metaphor of seasons changing and the repetitive cycles of life are present in this section. They embody encouragement because the dark days of winter are always, *always,* followed by the renewal and rebirth of spring.

The Possibility section contains prayers that offer a new way of thinking and a world where unity with universal knowing is easy and joyous. These prayers are particularly useful when I am looking for a way to break well-worn thought patterns, when my mind repeats with negative messages like "Oh, I can't do that," "I don't have the money for that idea," and "I won't be attractive to that person."

This section offers prayers as positive substitutions for the litany of can't, don't, won't, and shouldn't thoughts that can generate a negative energy and life of their own. Maybe, just maybe, there is another possible outcome to my patterned way of thinking. In the possibility of that thought, insert a prayer and see where it takes you!

I want to include a few words here about the use of the word "God" throughout this book, and a brief history of my lifelong journey to define my spiritual beliefs.

The prayers often include the work and language of times when I identified primarily as:

* a feminist practicing Wiccan spirituality;
* a goddess worshipper, where using the word "God" would have invoked a nod to the patriarchy in a negative way;
* an "earth mother" who prayed to Father Sky and Mother Earth, and
* a twelve-step believer, which suited me because I had only to believe in a power greater than myself and could call it anything I wanted. I methodically went through the beginning chapters of my first twelve-step book and every time the word "God" was used, I crossed it out and wrote "Higher Power." It was within the rooms of twelve-step

meetings that I again learned to invoke prayer for assistance in my daily life by falling in love with the simplicity and clarity of the Serenity Prayer.

Using the word "God" to identify the spiritual source from which I was seeking assistance did not fit for me at that time in my life. I had been raised in a relatively conservative, traditional Christian community. I was not sure then what or who I believed God to be, or even if I believed God existed. I knew that I did not agree with some of the patriarchal, judgmental, and punitive aspects that characterized "God" in the religious community of small-town Iowa. As a result, I developed reactivity to the word itself. So, I chose to replace "God" with various other words and concepts throughout the years that followed.

In the late '70s I prayed to the goddess, in the '80s and '90s to a higher power, at the beginning of the twenty-first century to the universe, source, spirit and guardian angels. All the while, I was feeling ever-closer to what so many religions call "God" and appreciating the simplicity of using that one single word. For me the word "God" has become a representation of love and my ability to see the best in myself and others.

As I was preparing the compilation of prayers for this manuscript, I was surprised at how many prayers spoke of GOD. This could not be true! I could not have written these. And why was the word GOD in all capitals?

As I continued writing, I came to understand. First, many of the prayers and affirmations in this compilation were written as gifts or at the request of clients. The language sometimes

changed, but the wording came as the best way to communicate the message for the intended recipient of the gift.

I also grew to understand that when I was writing the word GOD in all capitals, it was intended to mean something greater than a religious god. It was the expression of all that is good and all that is love. As this awareness began to take hold in me, I also realized that the word "god" holds nothing negative for me at this stage in my life. I believe in the nurturing and healing power of love and if GOD is a word that represents that, I happily offer it.

I encourage all who find their way to these prayers to rewrite them on your own cards for your daily use, substituting whatever language invokes love, joy, and ease.

I hope you will also do the same for the closing devotional statements. I first learned the devotional phrase "and so it is" at the Center for Spiritual Living. I love the intention and clarity of this phrase. It fits with my beliefs about the laws of attraction: manifesting and creating a life based on my best visualizing abilities.

I was raised using "amen" as the closing devotional statement to prayer. Along my path I have also been taught "blessed be" and "thank you" as the perfect closing to blessings or prayers.

Please use whatever is right for you. The purpose and intent of the prayers will not be altered by adjusting the language or gender. They are offered as gifts. I hope you will personalize them, love them, be inspired by them, and use them to enhance your life and fill your soul with love.

And so it is.

Comfort

Comfort

In joy and love I am comforted.
In happiness I am surrounded.

I am whole.
I am safe.
I am loved.

Attracting a future vibrating to my highest good
and the highest good of those I attract.

All is well and right with GOD.

    And so it is.

Instruction

When the whirl of life is spinning
and thoughts race along a well-worn path,

Sit down.
Take a breath.
Say a prayer.
Ask for peace.

When a heartache arrives like lightening and pulls you off
your feet,

Stand still.
Close your eyes.
Breathe deep.
Invoke the spirit helpers.
Ask for strength.

When the truth of self is all your soul can see,

Lie down.
Hear the music.
Feel your breath.
Trust the universe.

Experience love.

Always Rest First

The rhythms of life are easiest to manage
if we rest first.

When the waves are crashing,
the winds are blowing,
and the firewood seems very far away,
surround yourself in blankets
and rest first.

For in the resting space
the list diminishes and
the ego thoughts disappear.

The universe can step in
and manage processes and timing,
prosperity and connections.

In the resting space,
problems dissolve
and possibilities abound
as the guides, angels, and ancestors meet
to conspire for our greatest good.

Tend the fire.
Create a meal.
Feed the dog.
Finish the list.

But first,
curl up with your highest self
and rest.

Peace and Calm

Just for today,
I am at peace.

Just for today,
all my needs are met, and my family is healthy.

God is solving all my problems.

I will know the solutions when I need them.
All is well.

　　　And so it is.

Blossoming

I am filled with peace and confidence.
My journey is perfect and unfolding in GOD's time
in order to lead my spiritual growth.

I trust GOD.
I trust love.
I trust myself.

　　　And so it is.

Preparation

I ask and I receive.
My task is to prepare and respond
while I develop
faith, patience and love.

The light of God surrounds me and all I love.
My soul is peaceful,
knowing God's arms hold me
God's angels surround me and
my guides protect me.

Timing, resources, guidance, and love
are flowing perfectly to and from me
on each step of the journey
to becoming my true self.

And so it is.

Slow Down

I am a perfect child of GOD
and an imperfect human.

Both are joyfully true.

I am good and responsible and free.

All is right in GOD's time
and in Earth's time.

As I slow my pace, I will find peace.
I am GOD.
I am love.
I am peace.

All is well
today and every day.

Knowing

My love,
my joy,
my heart,
are in my hands and in my control.

I allow space easily.
My needs are met.
I am loved!

Divine Timing

I am never alone.

My divine plan
and the divine timing of all things is unfolding perfectly.

Everything I need is before me and beauty surrounds me.

I am safe.
I am loved.
I am GOD's beautiful child.

    And so it is.

Traveler

I am surrounded by safety, ease, and light.

My journey is led by my highest good and my choices
each day serves this purpose and this purpose only.

The people, places, and guides I meet
reflect love, security, beauty, and abundance.

I live in the light.
I attract only light.
I am free.

　　And so it is.

Releasing Fear

As the light returns to the earth,
so does it return to my soul.

There is nothing to fear that can be seen,
and I see fully and completely.

My life is perfect.

I attract health and prosperity daily,
as I release fear.

All is well.
I am love.

    And so it is and always will be.

Acceptance

I am exactly where I need to be,
doing exactly what I need to be doing.

My inner voices are voices of love and patience,
kindness and forgiveness.

All I have to be is what I am right now.

    And so it is.

Loving Another

May GOD hold you in the arms of love,
keep your soul safe from darkness
and your mind clear.

I ask you be surrounded with light.
I ask you be surrounded by love.
I ask for your thoughts and actions
to be aligned with GOD's will.

    And so it is.

Healing

Today I am filled with gratitude.
My body is healing.
I flow easily with the motions of life, and
I understand the importance
of surrendering to the divine timing
of health,
vitality,
and joy.

I live in God's house.
I have faith.

I trust in God's ability to relieve my worries,
to attune my fears to health,
and to transform my pain to wellness.

All is well
today and forever more.

    And so it is.

Full Moon Prayer

As I stand at the entrance
moving one foot and then the next,

I know who I am.
I know what my heart yearns to experience.

The seasons of grief are ending.
The seasons of rest and aloneness are ending.
The seasons of fear and uncertainty are ending.

As the moon passes fullness, I release.
And ask for the era of truth and clarity to begin.

I attract happiness.
I experience wealth.
I feel health.

My path forward is truly and undoubtedly
illuminating brightly.

    And so it is.

Forgiveness

I awaken to knowing I am free.
My thoughts,
my angers,
my grievances and sorrows
are all free to transform.

I can forgive now.
It is safe to turn my head,
to raise my arms and say
"It is done".

There are layers of story to unravel
about gods and angels and ancestors and
how they failed to do their job.

About others I have loved and faithfully adored
who did not return in kind.

About myself and how deeply wrong and flawed I have been.

It is done.
I am free to forgive.
I am able to heal.
I am forgiven this day and always.

    And so it is.

The Break-up

I am ready for peace.
I know in my heart I loved well
and provided for our love perfectly.

I release this relationship surrounded in love.
I am perfect
and a loving messenger of GOD.

I am grateful for all that this soul has been to me
and all that I am because of our love.

We are free.
I am content.
I separate filled with peace,
acceptance,
and love for myself.

All is well.

   And so it is.

Transition

My life transition occurs with ease
as I allow comfort and support from friends and family.

Divine timing is perfect timing, and
I am flowing awake.

I see my future.
It is filled with love,
connection, and partnership.

I have my heart's desire!

And so it is.

Self-Love

As I learn to forgive myself
All is well.

I am free to see myself
through the eyes of love
and
happiness
and
freedom.

My journey on earth is meant to be fun,
a time when I can skip and play,
laugh and make love,
sing and run,
and raise my arms to GOD
and say "Thank you!"

I am free.
I am joy.
I am love.

    And so it is.

Earthquake

There is a shaking occurring.
Shaking you loose and
inviting change.

When the earthquake of self
sends a repeating call,
Release.
Let go.
Curl under a tented table and wait.

The ego is shattering.
Breaking into Spirit
and creating a new self
built on character, integrity, confidence, and love.

The body is howling to the woods,
asking coyote and wolf to carry the carcass
and transform it through movement to grace and beauty.

The land has cracked open
and the crevice of spirit is shining through rocks
and shards of black onyx and gold.

Follow this new path to wholeness.
Release the tented life of security and obligation
to explore where spirit leads.

Crack open to good.
Crack open to possibility.
Crack open to the desires of your heart.

Crack open to love.

Alcohol

For my friends whose love affair
with alcohol is the GOD you understand,
may you find a new home in the arms
of love and the heart of peace.

While the detoxing thoughts of shame
and remorse and regret
pull you toward liquid courage,
may you find solace in kindness
and confidence, in grace and forgiveness.

Fill your broken places with jewels and
gemstone beads and molten steel.
Create mirrors with mosaic borders of every
"could have" and
"should have" and
"why didn't I" that you can gather.

See yourself belonging

to the spirit friends
who hold knowing,

to the earth friends
who hold woundedness,

to the water friends
who hold storytelling,

and to the fire friends
    who transform us all.

You are beautiful
and can rest in the freedom of knowing

you are good
and worthy
and whole.

  And so it is.

Crisis

In the alarm
every cell of my being is awake.
Cracked open.
On red alert.

As the information comes,
I understand the truth of all my fears.
Crashing like wild waves in a winter storm.

The gift of opportunity may come later.
The brutal shock of truth is all there is now.

And so we breathe,
In and out,
yielding to the rawness of this news.

We ask the angels of universal love
to hold a constant hover,
and
when the words and the wailing stop,

it is my GOD and my self alone,
reckoning,
integrating awake.

Relationships End

You have been gone for days now.
First, I pray for your safety and health.

Next, I pray for you to arrive at a place of self-forgiveness.
A place where you can honor our love and friendship.
A place where you hold me with love and respect.

I am in the release-and-cleanse process,

releasing you to GOD and cleansing my home,
my thoughts,
my psyche.

I am complete.
Our love is honored and returned to a pure and honest state.
There will be no going back now.

I am grounded and whole and able to move forward
to wealth
and love
and sexual satisfaction
and partnership.
Fully, happily, and peacefully.

Good-bye.
Be well.
Be good to yourself.

May you find the path to become your best self.

And so it is and always will be.

When Our Sisters Die

Death has arrived at our darkest season.
My soul weeps for this loss.
And
my soul rejoices in tears for my sister as she learns to fly.

My heart aches with sadness as I reflect on a life and its complexity.
The sister of soul lives on in me, yet the wound of my heart engulfs hope and surrender.

My heart has returned to a cocoon state to be still.
Emergence will arrive as a chrysalis in spring and butterfly in summer.

Threads of karma and lifetime pacts are unwinding and releasing in my body.
I will dance them free as the seasons change.

Today I feel,
I express,
I rest,
and I heal.

A scar has formed from this loss
a gift of living and loving well.

Today
I release any fear, guilt, shame, or remorse I carry as a sister.

I am beautiful.
I love completely.

My sister lives in me
and through me
and for me
always and forever more.

And so it is.

Grief

When grief is all there is,
allow space for memories of joy and serenity
to float beside such deep emotion.

Our lives are imprinted by those we love.
The gift of love deepens our sorrow and
lightens our pain.

Know that our souls are always connected
in heavens and beyond.

There is only love
and gratitude
and forgiveness.

You are blessed.
You may find peace.
You are so very loved,

now and forever more.

    And so it is.

Our Blessed Companions

Beloved creature,
our souls connect
as you rise to a home in GOD space.

Your precious face forever smiling,
youthful and free.

You have been a blessed companion,
and I release you.

You have been a great protector,
and I release you.

You have been a tender love,
and I release you.

Go forth, knowing we are connected
and whole
and complete.

I hold you in my heart.
See you in my dreams.
Feel you in the essence of my being.

All is well.

And so it is.

Bless and Release the Animals

My animal companion has been returned to Source.
My heart weeps for its loss.

I release all earthly thoughts of attachment
and accept the pure essence of our connection.

In GOD space we are united
by love,
by light,
and by joy,

now and forever more.

And so it is.

Presence of Calm

I pray for peace,
security,
and joy.

Calmness surrounds me and love abides.

All is well
as each piece of this human drama
unfolds exactly as it should.

The universe provides everything I need
at just the right time for my highest good
and the highest good of all involved,

always and forever more.

    And so it is.

Present Moment

I am whole.
I am perfect.
I am happy.

I pay attention every day
to what is right in front of me.

I know how to move forward confidently,
as I see my answers are in the present moment.

    And so it is.

Nothingness

Do not be afraid of the nothing space,
that space between what used to be
and what has not yet arrived.

This space is beautiful,
worthy of microscopic analysis
and deep, meditative breaths.

In the nothing space
everything is imaginable.
Synchronicity and serendipity,
coincidence and déjà-vu hold master classes.

The psychedelic subtleties of each unique life may be examined.

Nothingness exists to inspire us
and heal us
and guide us to love.

Embrace it.
Invite it.
Bless it.

Know yourself.

Love

As my mind begins to organize the day,
let it always land on love.

When my body sings a song of tired
or fills with ache and overwhelm,
let it find relief in love.

When my soul has wandered to a forest of loneliness
and questions
and "How?"
let it sit by the riverbank of love.

For in the presence of love, the solutions appear.
The problems dissolve.

The mind and body and soul are free and limitless,
magnificent,
majestic,
and calm.

Love is where we begin,
where we end,
and everything between.

And so it is.

Encouragement

Encouragement

I am a child of this universe.
I represent joy, connection, and possibility
in all that I do.

My highest good reveals itself to me
at a pace,
and in the sequence,
that is exactly right for all involved.

I am safe.
I am whole.
I am loved.

And so it is.

Woman's Credo

I know who I am and what I want.
When I create moments of stillness
I am able to see myself and my life clearly.

As a mother I commit to fun,
happiness and enjoyment
of each stage of growth and love.

As a woman I commit to health,
beauty and ease
at loving and nurturing myself.

As a partner I commit to health
and goals that serve ourselves and our family.

I am equal and whole,
loving and kind,
giving and receiving.

As a daughter I am whole and wise,
expressing love and gratitude
in all that I do.

I ask forgiveness.
I receive abundance.
I live in gracious and prosperous wholeness.

    And so it is.

Morning Prayer

Every morning I can choose
the best use of my time, my thoughts,
my money, and my energy
for this day.

And every evening I will know who I am,
what I need, and
how to proceed.

I am grateful.
I am confident.
I am complete.

And so it is.

Clarity

For today I have clarity.
I know who I am and what I need.

I am loved by GOD and
guided by spirits and angels
who move me toward my highest good.

I know how to love unconditionally,
while holding true to my needs, boundaries, and desires.

And so it is.

Arrival

The time is now
to be who I have always wanted to become.

I am a leader in my family,
a companion to my friends, and
an agent of truth to myself.

I am ready.
I have arrived.

The path is revealing itself,
sparkling with diamonds, rubies, and love.

Love is all I deliver and all I desire.
Thank you.

And so it is.

Readiness

Just like a drop of water in the pond,
one simple action
can change the course of nature.

I am ready.
I have everything I need.
The time is now.
Begin...

Forward

Today I move forward.

I am safe.
I am clear.
I know who I am and what I want.

Forgiveness,
trust,
faith, and
love come easily and frequently to my heart and soul.

    And so it is.

Faith

I am whole.

I am content.

I have faith in goodness and love.

I am guided and protected in all that I do,

today and all the days of my life.

Spirals

From the center of a spiral
I emerge.

Winding out of a long pathway
built for protection,
and safety,
and stillness.

Emerging greets and releases fear,
greets and releases enough,
greets and releases uncertainty.

Arrival welcomes balance,
clarity, and love.

It begins with love.
It is love.
It ends with love.

I am loved.

And so it is.

Just Right

Everything is just right
always.

Especially when the moon is dim
and the darkness creates shadow
of confusion,
uncertainty,
and wallowing.

Everything is just right,
falling into place
in tiny detail.

Pull back, dear one.
See the whole.

See the brilliant picture coming into view.
Breathe.
Have faith.
Trust.

In The Flow

Flowing downstream
in the river of life,
I see the fine details
and the tiny pieces clearly.

As thoughts come,
I release them to GOD and my highest self.

I ask for them to be washed anew,
and for new pathways of the highest order
to be lit with luminaries
and glisten with detail.

There are no mistakes.

As I move perfectly
to the sounds of
abundance,
joy,
prosperity,
and love.

    And so it is.

Equinox

The season is here for renewal and peace.
My task is listening and my gift is clarity.
I ask for energy,
play, and
rejuvenation.

I can work and feel happy at day's end.
I can play and have energy for work.

My spirit is light.
My days are balanced.
My journey is easy.

And so it is.

Spring

I am alive with possibility and joy.
Just as the birdsong flows,
so does my heart's desire.

I am healed.
I am washed anew.
I am walking confidently to my future.

    And so it is.

Autumn

As the season changes,
so do I.

My worries and habits fall away like leaves
and I am filled with ideas and energy.

I understand what my body needs for health.
I choose slow and steady changes
to support constant well-being.

Peace.
Choice.
Movement.

    And so it is.

Winter Solstice

As the light returns,
so does energy and zest for life.

I am ready to commit to my home,
my work,
and my routine
as complete, rejuvenating, and correct.

People, activity, and fun
occur easily and frequently now.

I embrace newness.
I love my life.
I invite the unknown with ease and grace.

And so it is.

Holiday Season

In the season of giving I see clearly
how much I have,
how much I give,
and how much I aspire to achieve.

I always have more than enough
and joyfully provide safety, security, play, and surprise for my
family.

Today is the day to express gratitude for what I have,
what I give, and what I receive.
The flow of money and resources endlessly arrive
in ways beyond my imagination.

I am free to be happy and to joyfully create my future.
I am free to enjoy life.
I owe nothing.

My happiness, my prosperity, and my freedom are a gift
from GOD,
with no beginning and no end.
I am grateful.

　　And so it is.

Renewal

Renewal is alive in me
as it is in the earth.

There is a plan.
I am on the path.

Health,
joy,
relief,
and possibility
are plentiful and never-ending.

I believe.
I am love.
I am good.

    And so it is.

Please

Please help me to feel relaxed
and easy about my future.

Reveal enough
for my confidence
and my heart's desire
to soar forward.

I am love and ease.
I am grace and peace.
I am grateful and complete.

And so it is and always will be.

Health

Today I begin my future.

Whole,
content, and
clear.

My food is fuel.
My health is perfect.
My body is strong and flexible.

I know how.

    And so it is.

Money Magnet

I am a money magnet and money loves me.

I flow with abundance beyond my wildest dreams
attracting wealth, joy, and possibility in each moment.

I am guided toward my best future
in each step I take,
each call I make, and
each idea I pursue.

I listen to my inner voice and trust my intuition
as I navigate the white waters of uncertainty.

I am whole.
I am perfect.
I am love.

> And so it is.

Attracting Love

My body is strong,
my heart is tender, and
my arms are stretched in reach for a soul connection.

My task is love
Right here.
Right now.

Release to GOD and the source of all that is good.

The time for peace is now.
The time for joy is now.
The time for love is right now.

Be the lover and the friend.
Heal.
Be still.
Listen.

> And so it is.

Dating

GOD
I am willing and able to set my fears aside
and welcome the perfect date.

Please send a date who is available,
single,
and the right match for me,
today and into the future.

I forgive myself.
My past is the experience I use to create my future.
My heart is open.
I am ready.

> And so it is.

New Love

I am whole.
I am content.

I care for my own needs as partnership begins.

It is from this place of wholeness
that love, relationship, and sexual union occur.

GOD's time is the only correct time.

Correct time is the only right time for me.

> And so it is.

Conception

The time is now,
as our souls are ready to receive.

We are united and joyful,
calm, and secure.

Conception of life,
of love,
of family,
and of connection
is our dream and our purpose together.

And so it is.

Soul Calling

As I make a call to GOD and the
universal source of Divine Love
my future unfolds.

I am relaxed.
I am free.
I am peaceful and fully alive.

Three souls have joined
and ask for the unique energy made just for them
to come to earth and join this life.

We are ready.
We are here to be your parents.
We are love.

As GOD prepares the timing,
we release all attachments to time, gender, space and beloved
control.

We allow space for GOD's timing.
We allow space for GOD's grace.
We allow space for GOD's love.

Our future is lined with jewels, bedazzled with angel wings and
illuminated by love.

GOD's time is our time.

And so it is.

Unconditional Love

When a child has chosen you to love,
pay attention,
this gift is precious and true.

Walk hand in hand,
sit heart to heart,
listen soul to soul,
as the journey is now sealed.

The cords of fate
and the orchestra of destiny
have created a symphony so powerful,
the deepest truest love exists here
and only here.

Rejoice and offer thanks
the child has chosen you.

Blessed be.

Choosing My Path

I choose my destiny.
I choose my path.

Roadblocks disappear
and solutions become obvious
as I move toward my true knowing.

Good begets good
and right action cannot be questioned.

I know who I am.
I know what I want.
I approve of my actions.

    And so it is.

Liminal Space

Do not change course now!
You have earned and deserve the future awaiting you.

It is worth it!
You have created it!

You will be filled with joy and wonder.

Do not turn back now,
as the hard work is done.

It is spirit and faith now.
You have arrived.
You are whole.
You are healed.

Relax and enjoy.

Bask in your light
and the light of GOD shining through you,
now and forever more.

Designing Life

My life is filled with joy and ease.
I have created exactly the life necessary
to support my highest good.

I deserve peace.
I deserve prosperity.
I am love.

The Universe can only provide what I can imagine.
Therefore,
I look for possibility
in my every thought and action.

And so it is.

Tuesday Morning

My future is unfolding
right before my eyes
and all is well.

As I see clearly
I take a step.

When the path is fogged over
or the light is a twilight hue,
I wait.

At each juncture,
in the present moment,
I know.

As I experience faith and health,
confidence,
peace, and joy
I move to the next brick.

Taking the next step
to the greatest path this life can offer.

Self awareness.
Self expression.
Self love.

And so it is.

Helping

Today I help from a place of
self-love and self-care.

My gifts flow easily to others
when I am filled with love, generosity, and peace.

All that I am and
all that I do is whole and beautiful,
as I give to others and then know
it is enough.

When I offer assistance
I provide one thing,
carefully planned and prepared
from my heart space and in GOD's time.

I take a breath and receive all that I need.

The circle of giving and receiving
creates a rainbow of energy that sustains me,
heals me, and
holds me in the arms of GOD.

All is well today and every day.

I am perfect.
I am whole.
I am complete.

    And so it is.

All Is Well

All is well with my friends and my family.

Each person I love and each person they love
are walking perfectly on their own path of destiny,
as am I.

When we are connected by love and acceptance
I have no need to judge or worry.

I release thoughts of concern,
and replace them with thoughts of grace and compassion.

There are no mistakes in GOD's plan.

As we each manifest the life lessons necessary
to achieve our highest good,
we are carried in the arms of love and faith and hope.

    And so it is.

A Grateful Heart

Today I have a grateful heart,
for blessings and challenges,
nourishment and desire.

A grateful heart beats to the sounds of nature
and flows in fresh air.

When I receive my day in gratefulness,
my worries become small
and the gifts of life are all I can see.

As I take this moment to stop
and speak from a grateful heart,
my list is long and pure and beautiful.

I have a grateful heart.

I am grateful for this day
to live,
to love,
to experience joy.

Blessed be.

Possibility

Possibility

As I take time for day dreams and wandering
I can see underneath the shimmering water
and the pools that catch a waterfall.

The elements show themselves as sprite and nymph,
phoenix and Pegasus and fire dragon.

The trees and streams offer a world for fairies and pixies,
trolls, hobbits and gnomes.

Go outside dear ones.
Listen.
Find them.
See beyond the literal and explore your creative source.

The soils of Mother Earth contain a story
of death and rebirth,
of growth and renewal
and nature's ability to prune.

There is a land beyond the veil of literal.
Dwell there each day.
Experience your heart as free.

Blessed be.

Gifts from Guidance

There is a place in our inner landscape
That knows only of wholeness and love and faith.

When we meet in this place
the possibilities of life are endless,
the solutions appear with brilliant light and clarity.

Follow a path or a meandering river to find this land
and stay true to the song of your own heart.

The guides speak only of love
and possibility
and infinite joy.

Holding the highest truth and deepest love
as you journey forward.

Listen to the space between your breaths,
become lovers with quiet and calm,
taste the colors of nature,
then… soar above it all and see perfection.

We meet in this spirit-filled space
and offer gifts of wealth and jewels for love;
staff and crowns and robes for peace.

You are majestic,
royal,
whole,
and unique.

Be guided to your gifts with ease and grace.

Spiritual Sisters

Today I speak to myself as I speak
to the young ones.

Living with an open heart is a beautiful way to live,
where all the colors are known and each depth is felt.

A wide open life is not for the faint of heart or the wounded.
It is for us,
the strong,
vibrant,
joyful ones.

The ones who love deeply and
who live in passion and kindness and purpose.

Be a woman who loves with an open heart - as I am.
Be a woman who risks it all for tenderness
and kisses
and dreams.

Be strong like me.
Be kind like me.
Be whole like me.

And so it is.

True and Authentic Self

Today is the day for action.
My thoughts,
my body, and
my emotions are in alignment,
as I explore
the essence of being my true and authentic self.

I ask for connection,
expression,
and movement with joy.

I love life.
I love money.
I love being free.

On this day
and in this moment,
I am free
and express myself easily, happily, and energetically.

And so it is.

Heart's Desire

I enter into a space of personal clarity today.
Where worries and fears,
uncertainty and pressure
do not exist.

I draw to myself images, baubles and experiences
that inspire my inner joy and happiness.

In GOD's space I am free to play
and explore
and become my truest self.

And so it is.

Birthday Prayer

I celebrate my life in all that I do
and all who I love know the truth of my heart.

I create a glorious world,
where the dreams of my future
manifest in my daily life.

I am whole.
I am love.
I am secure.

There is no waiting for brilliance and love.

The year before me is already blessed to my highest good
with health,
partnership,
happiness, and
prosperity.

I have all that I need.
I have all that I desire.

    And so it is.

Daughters

The reflection of daughters is a journey across
lifetimes that tell of the lines on our faces,
the creases on our hands,
and the silhouette of our shape.

The daughters hold gentleness
and power
and always the naked truth
of who we are,
who our parents imprinted us to be
and how the ancestors dreamed us all into possibility.

Our greatest gift to offer them is loving ourselves,
as they see themselves reflected through us.

The daughters are magnificent
and brave,
vulnerable and wise and
ripe with everything we have yet to accomplish.

Love is always enough.

    And so it is.

Crazy Love

In the eyes and arms of a grandchild
I understand crazy love,
a place where love is free, easy, calm, and precious.

I am my best self in crazy love.
There is nowhere else I am meant to be,
nothing I am meant to do.

The truth of life exists here as unconditional facts of happiness.

In crazy love every single thing is interesting,
the beginning of a creative story
or a mud pie while gardening.
A dance to the bird feeder
as a lyrical tune of life's simplest moments.

Look Grandpa!
Come see Grandma!
Let me show you the fairies and angels
and the deepest truth of what is important.

Crazy love has healed me, humbled me,
and brought me to my highest and best self.

In the child's eyes I know peace.
In the child's arms my heart is healed of every loving wound.
In the child's heart I can sing and play, dance and rejoice in
freedom.

Crazy love has saved me,
renewed my faith, and taught me hope.

In crazy love I know the universe is a loving place,
where I am perfect
and all is well,
truly and absolutely.

And so it is.

Creativity

The artist arises
and all is well.

The gift flows through me
from a place of divine perfection.

I connect to love as my compass
and
live inspired.

Prosperity illuminates my path and
paints my future.

I am love.
I am GOD.
I am well.

And so it is.

Butterfly

I have learned and now I practice.
I have seen and now I know.
I am complete and perfect.

As I fall into the arms of GOD
peace,
tranquility, and
curiosity abound.

The shimmering world is open to my exploration and
cocooning is complete.
Chrysalis now.

As GOD - So Am I.

Opportunity

The Universe is filled with opportunity for me.

As I relax into knowing abundance
I will see it vibrating to me in a thousand ways.

I release attachment.
I release fear.

I attract thoughts, feelings, actions, and people
who represent my highest good.

And so it is.

Abundance

I am abundant in every way possible
and attract wealth,
security,
safety, and
love in all of my relationships.

As I radiate joy and abundance
it becomes all that I see.

And so it is.

Summer

The earth and moon are synchronized
for summer's arrival
and the rebirth of our lives.

As I look around
I see clearly who I am,
how I create,
and what I know.

This masterfully crafted life is brilliant
and perfect
and filled with abundance and love.

I am well.
I am lovely.
I am gentle and kind and beautiful.

And so it is.

Illumination

The path I have chosen is illuminated
and sparkling.
Diamonds, emeralds and topaz glisten
and twinkle as my future.

My gift is patience.
My path is study.
My calling is wealth.

I know who I am and why I am here.
Regardless of what I do,
in me is all that I need.

I am peace.
I am love.

And so it is.

Solstice Crone

The light has returned.
The chalice is full and I am ready
to flow in
to a new phase.

I am a woman of strength
and power
and grace,
moving to a time of clarity and gift-giving.

I share openly with the young ones
to support and encourage.

I clarify the path of right action for some who are confused.
I give widely and easily as I become
the Elder,
the Crone,
the Healer.

　　And so it is.

Love and Gratitude

I ask for my path forward to be illuminated
with jewels and love.

I see clearly now,
who I am,
how I love, and
what I deserve.

I meet each day with gratitude and
openness to what is unknown and possible.

I am free.
I am joy.
I am attracting new love
and fulfilling my heart's desire.

All is perfect and flowing easily
to and from.

    And so it is.

Moving To My Future

Today I move forward.
I am safe.
I am clear.

I know who I am and what I want.

Forgiveness,
trust,
faith, and love
come easily and frequently
to my heart
and to my soul.

    And so it is.

Glowing

My essence is glowing.

Now is the time to integrate the lessons of parenting,
stress,
manifestation,
and dependence.

I am able.
I am ready.
Moving forward fully depends on my willingness.
This I understand and embrace.

    And so it is.

Self Esteem

I am a soul
in a human form.

I am never alone in spirit time.

My thoughts and my actions
are an expression of my love for myself,
my care for myself, and
my approval of all that is.

Life is glorious and I embrace each experience as a gift.
I hold my hands open,
my heart as joyful, and
my body as relaxed.

When I see myself as spirit sees me
I know the brilliance of my being,
the uniqueness of my gifts, and
the sparkling perfection of my nature.

The universe has imprinted me for delight
and happiness
and love!

And so it is.

Perfection

Perfection already exists.
As I surrender to this knowing
my goals are achieved.

My life is a reflection of my thoughts.
My thoughts reflect my heart's desire.

As I embrace and control my thoughts,
my life becomes my heart's desire.

    And so it is.

Cocooning

As I release pursuit of perfection
I find energy,
curiosity, and love
surround me with no effort or plan.

I am a student of life
and I am requesting an
education of the highest order.

As I learn to become my best and highest self,
the act of doing falls away and
the chrysalis of my true self appears.

I am surrounded with love
and the light of GOD always.

    And so it is.

Chrysalis

I have learned and now I practice.
I have seen and now I know.

I am complete and perfect.
As I fall into the arms of GOD
peace,
tranquility,
and curiosity abound.

The shimmering world
is open to my exploration.

Cocooning is complete.
Chrysalis now.

As GOD so am I.

Surrender

I release all control
and
surrender to peace,
faith,
trust,
and confidence.

It is the season for clarity and action
for my health,
for my family,
for my love.

I surrender everything
and ask that it be
built anew for my greatest good.

I am love.
I feel free.
I choose myself.
It has begun.

    And so it is.

Service

Please offer me as an instrument
of peace and calm.
I deepen learning for others while
knowing myself.

I am whole.
I am GOD.
I am love.

    And so it is.

True Calling

You are a beloved child of God.
As you flourish,
your ability to reach toward the light
and true calling of your soul
will shine brightly.

    And so it is.

Prosperity

I am joyfully prepared.
Tending money is a playful and exciting part of my day.

I have endless time and energy to
give,
receive,
track, and
multiply dollars
all day long.

The flow of prosperity is alive
and shimmering with generosity
and goodness in my being.

And so it is.

Divine Guidance

Abundance is all I understand or attract.
Relaxation and calm are all I desire.

The flow of energy from the Universe
goes to and through me with ease.

As I stay in the river of divine guidance,
divine timing, and
answered prayers
I am one with universal power.

My thoughts are surrounded always with love
and tuned to the highest good for all.

    And so it is.

The Journey

My journey is now.

I have all that I need.
I am all that I can be.
Right now,
today
I am free.

I release and flow with the
universal current of abundance,
clarity, and love.

There is no place but here.
No time but now.
No life but mine.

Create – Dream – Grow.

    And so it is.

Happiness

Faith, love, and happiness are my heart's desire.

As I find my new centered way
with these actions as my compass,

I breathe.
I relax.
I trust.

All is well and always will be.
My life is spirit led and divinely guided.

Every day in every way
now and forever more.

    And so it is.

A Peaceful Day

Today is a peaceful day.

I carry peace in the melodies of my mind,
the gait of my walk,
and the sounds of my voice.

I arise each morning to greet the day with ease.
As I express gratitude,
faith,
and enthusiasm
I begin my daily rituals.

I awaken my body with a stretch and a smile
as I prepare fuel for the day,
cleansing with water the worries and fear dreams of the darkness.

I awaken my emotions with a prayer and a request
for ease,
and love,
and simple happiness in each moment.

I awaken my spirit with expressions of gratitude for all I receive
and forgiveness for my human failings.
Asking for creativity,
and hope,
and confidence to guide my soul's work.

And last, I awaken my thoughts.
Inviting them to hover in affirmation of my future
as filled with wealth,
and kindness,
and grace.

Today is a peaceful day.
A blissful day.
A perfect day.

And so it is.

Authentic Beauty
What Sustains Me?

Inside I am lovely,
delicious, and free.

I am sustained by the lines on my face
and the wrinkles on my hands.
They are born of surviving grief,
the healing of shame, and
the beauty of forgiveness
in all possible forms.

Directing me through seasons
and moons,
and generations of ancient voices
and
drumming that beats my heart
and lifts my spirit.

Call my name in the wind,
in the deep water,
and the embers of fire and earth.

I am sustained by knowing my true self
as whole
and perfect
and lovely.

Acknowledgements

The prayers and affirmations included in **Gifts From Guidance** have come as a part of my personal journey to create a spirit-led life. There are so many to acknowledge and to whom I express my considerable gratitude and appreciation. I hope I have told you along the way what you mean to me.

For Jenifer

My best friend, business partner, and trusted confidante.
Your life journey is woven in these pages alongside mine, as our paths are joined. It is through you and your family that I have learned patience, kindness, acceptance, and the healing power of love.

This book exists because of you.
Thank you. A thousand times over, thank you!

For Emily

I love you and believe you are perfect exactly as you are.
Our souls are intertwined on a karmic path that certainly spans lifetimes. This time, I am the mother, yet you are so often my teacher and guide.

Through my love for you, I have learned how to act from my highest self more frequently and to release a generational pattern of codependency and obsessive worrying. This personal journey in our relationship has created the healing space and time necessary for me to write this book.

You are a gift to me.
Everyday.
  Always.

Abigail Kay Jones

This past year of writing has also been a year of taking you to-and-from preschool three days every week. I have shared the journey of writing this book, with you, more often than anyone else. During this time, you have created your own desk space, prepared three-ring binders of colored paper, created collages, complete with glue and scissors and glitter – lots of glitter, and assisted me with paper hole-punching each draft, along with organizing the office supplies.

I adore you and appreciate everything you show me of love, kindness, and a four year old's curiosity and world view. You have kept me grounded and helped me to believe in myself by telling me the stories of your day and the simplicity of your love for me. Thank you for choosing me to love and inspiring the prayer *Crazy Love*!

For Amy

My soul-connected friend and colleague.
You showed me the incredible ways these prayers can transform suffering, heartache, and fear in real life… truly transform an experience.

Your faith in me is unparalleled.
I thank you so much.

Jennifer Kuhns

The artwork for this book is perfect. It is exactly what I did not know I was asking for until you tenderly and carefully supported me to see the image! Your talent as a mosaic artist is exceptional and I thank you so much for guiding me through the artistic process of creating such a beautiful piece of art.

Our success is intertwined and I am forever grateful to you for inspiring me.

Mitch Teufel, Mary Ann Naughton, Jan Secor, Gail Fairfield, Jennefer Blinstrub, Jodi Watson, Christine Buckley and **Dan R.**

You have each taught me, challenged me, loved me, believed in me, and inspired me as I developed the ability to create this book. Your imprints are embedded in my story and in the prayers. As I say "thank you" my heart is full of happiness and love.

About the Author

Kay Christy lives and works in the Pacific Northwest in a beautiful community nestled at the base of Puget Sound. She has crafted her heart's-desire life, which includes time for loving, writing, working, and being a devoted and engaged grandparent.

A graduate of The Evergreen State College, she holds an MA degree in behavioral science from the Leadership Institute of Seattle (LIOS). In addition to her formal education, she has been a student and practitioner of metaphysics and the intuitive arts for the past thirty-five years.

In 2012, she created the Spirit Led Life Company (www.SpiritLedLifeCompany.com) to house her signature products and services, with the intention of supporting people in designing a joy-filled and peaceful life. Many of the products sold by Spirit Led Life Company are inspired by the prayers and affirmations in this book.

The services Kay offers in private practice are three-pronged,

* She works with individuals as a personal effectiveness coach, which includes writing personalized prayers and affirmations to enhance her clients' spiritual development. The synchronicity that occurs by combining the behavioral science techniques of life coaching with the intuitive arts never ceases to surprise and delight both Kay and her clients.

* As a small business development consultant, she teaches and consults with business owners, entrepreneurs, and private practitioners. Her unique niche is incorporating spiritual principles with sound business management and marketing tools.
* She occasionally performs organization development consulting in the form of leadership development training and executive coaching, particularly where leaders and managers are interested in incorporating spiritual principles into their daily work routines.